Critical reading of <u>Flight Behavior</u>

by Barbara Kingsolver

from a Unitarian Universalist's perspective

By David G. Markham

Essay 1

Do people want to do the right environmental thing or make money?

Lester R. Brown asks in his essay, "Ecopsychology and the Environmental Revolution" in the book, Ecopsychology: Restoring The Earth, Healing The Mind, "Do we believe people want to do the right environmental thing? Do we believe people care about the future of the living planet? Ecopsychologists believe there is an emotional bond between human beings and the natural environment out of which we evolve." p. xvi

I think Brown puts his last sentence in the quote a bit clumsily. There is no emotional bond between human beings and the natural environment because human beings are part of the natural environment whether they like it or not because of the air they breathe, the water they drink, the ground they pee and poop on.

As James Hillman writes in the next essay in the same book, "A Psyche the Size of the Earth," "Psychology, so dedicated to awakening the human consciousness, needs to wake itself up to one of the most ancient human truths: we cannot be studied or cured apart from the planet." p. xxii

This month, July, 2014, we will be reading and discussing Barbara Kingsolver's book, Flight Behavior, which grapples with these theological and psychological questions in the microcosm of the life of the Turnbow family in the Appalachian mountains of Tennesee. Here is a blurb from the Amazon web site:

Flight Behavior is a brilliant and suspenseful novel set in present day Appalachia: a breathtaking parable of catastrophe and denial that explores how the complexities we inevitably encounter in life lead us to believe in our particular chosen truths. Kingsolver's riveting story concerns a young wife and mother on a failing farm in rural Tennessee who experiences something she cannot explain, and how her discovery energizes various competing factions—religious leaders, climate scientists, environmentalists, politicians—trapping her in the center of the conflict and ultimately opening up her world. *Flight Behavior* is arguably Kingsolver's must thrilling and accessible novel to date, and like so many other of her acclaimed works, represents contemporary American fiction at its finest.

The key event in Flight Behavior is the arrival of Monarch butterflies for a winter roost in the Turnbow woods when they normally go to Mexico where their habitat has been destroyed by symptoms of climate change.

Flight Behavior deals with elements of theology, psychology, sociology, ecology, biology and raises issues of our care of the planet, our Mother Earth, which we all must face if not in as an immediate and dramatic way.

Essay 2

Trees glowed with an orange blaze. "Jesus God", she said again.

Does it seem odd that Flight Behavior by Barbara Kingsolver was chosen as a book to discuss for a month on UU A Way Of Life? It won't once you realize that the story told in Flight Behavior exemplifies the application of UU's seventh principle, "respect for the interdependent web of all existence of which we are a part."

Actually you might read the book and come away impressed that Kingsolver is a very spiritual person. Her characters grapple with real life challenges in applying the UU seventh principle as the story unfolds.

Dellarobia Turnbow is a forlorn young woman who marries her high school sweetheart when she finds she is pregnant. However the baby is still born, and with the reason and purpose of the marriage no longer applicable, Dellarobia stays with husband, Cub, anyway and as the novel opens she has had two more children with him, and is unfaithful to him, and is on her way to a tryst with her lover when an amazing event occurs which changes the course of her life.

Dellarobio is hiking up a path in a forested area of the appalachian mountains in Tennessee behind her house to meet her lover in an old hunting cabin when she noticed unusual clumps of something on the trees and then:

"The forest blazed with its own internal flame. 'Jesus,' she said, not calling for help, she and Jesus weren't that close, but putting her voice in the world because nothing else present make sense. The sun slipped out by another degree, passing its warmth across the land, and the mountain seemed to explode with light. Brightness of a new intensity moved up the valley in a rippling wave, like the disturbed surface of a lake. Every bough glowed with an orange blaze. 'Jesus God,' she said again. No words came to her that seemed sane. Trees turned to fire, a burning bush. Moses came to mind, and Ezekiel, words from Scripture that occupied a certain space in her brain but no longer carried honest weight, if they ever had. *Burning coals of fire went up and down among the living creatures.*" p.14

What Dellabobia will eventually find out is that she is seeing Monarch butterflies, millions of them, coming to Tennessee for their winter roost instead of their usual winter roost in

Mexico because of climate change.

Human beings, in their hubris, think they have dominated and can control Mother Nature until Mother Nature teaches them different. It is humbling, staggering, maybe frightening, and we are left with nothing to say or think but "Jesus God" as Dellarobia did, even if we are not on good terms with either.

What we humans are doing to Mother Nature is horribly sinful and it has happened so slowly, unconsciously, incrementally since the beginning of the industrial age 200 years ago that we didn't even know what we were doing to our environment until now as the facts come in. As the symptoms of climate change are more apparent, and less deniable, we are left with Dellarobia with nothing to say but gasp "Jesus God".

Would that more of us on this planet would have a similar wake up experience and in our surprise awakening utter the same humble prayer. I haven't heard it uttered enough, and it is attention getting to read a fictional character utter it. Would that in our Unitarian Universalist churches, as we find our own examples of environmental change, we humbly pray to our Higher Power whatever we conceive of he/she/it or nothing to be, because we will need a lot of help to adjust to the consequences of the damage we have done. May God have mercy on us.

Galen Guengerich whose book, God Revised, was discussed on UU A Way Of Life last month suggested that a foundational ethic for a new religious movement might be gratitude. While that might be helpful, it is limited without repentance and acknowledgement of our sins which we have committed either knowingly or unknowingly, but what we knew and when we knew it, Mother Nature has no interest in. The bad karma is based on actions not necessarily intentional or malevolently motivated. Now that we know, to beg for mercy seems an appropriate response to the advancing environmental changes we will see with the terrible consequences for human beings and other living things.

"Jesus God", indeed.

Essay 3

Nature is not to be dominated because it is part of us and we part of her.

Dellarobia, standing on that mountain top, seeing the Monarch butterflies has a mystical experience of sorts. Kingsolver writes in her novel Flight Behavior:

"She (Dellarobia) is on her own here, staring at the glowing trees. Fascination curled itself around her fright. This is no forest fire. She was pressed by the quiet elation of escape and knowing better and seeing straight through to the back of herself, in solitude. She couldn't remember when she'd had such room for being. This was not just some fake thing in her life's cheap chain of events, leading up to this day of sneaking around in someone's thrown-away boots. Here that ended. Unearthly beauty had appeared to her, a vision of glory to stop her in the road. For her alone these orange boughs lifted, these long shadows became a brightness rising. It looked like the inside of joy, if a person could see that. A valley of lights, an ethereal wind. It had to mean something." p.15-16

Ikkyu, the Japaneese Zen Buddhist monk of the 15th century wrote "Every day, priests minutely examine the Law and endlessly chant complicated sutras. Before doing that, though, they should learn how to read the love letters sent by the wind and rain, the snow and moon."

Dellabrobia in pursuit of carnal love or more likely lust comes face to face the a "love letter" from Mother Nature. Such a love letter engenders a sense of awe, mystery, beauty.

Thomas Berry writes:

"When we first arrived as settlers, we saw ourselves as the most religious of peoples, as the most free in our political traditions, the most learned in our universities, the most competent on our technologies, and the most prepared to exploit every economic advantage. We saw ourselves as a divine blessing for this continent. In reality, we were a predator people on an innocent continent." p.17, "The World Of Wonder" in Spiritual Ecology.

We have been taught in our Judeo-Christian tradition that human beings are here to dominate the earth and so we have further developed a dichotomy of us and nature. Nature often is depicted as our enemy with forces to be tamed. Slowly we are realizing that we are not separate from nature but part of nature. There is no battle here, but a matter of cooperation and collaboration.

Chief Oren Lyons, the faithkeeper of the Turtle Clan of the Onondaga Nation writes:
"So I would say that in the ideas of renewing yourself and the ideas of finding peace in our community, you should tell your leaders and you should tell everybody that there can never be world peace as long as you make war against Mother Earth. To make war against Mother Earth is to destroy and to corrupt, to kill, to poison. When we do that, we will not have peace. The first peace comes with your mother, Mother Earth." p.11, "Listening to Natural Law" in Spiritual Ecology.

Dellabrobia is making peace with herself and her environment when she has a shift in perception, what in A

Course of Miracles, is called a miracle.

Miracle principle 29 is "Miracles praise God through you. They praise Him by honoring His creations, affirming their perfection. They heal because they deny body-identification and affirm spirit-identification."

Miracle principle 30 is "By recognizing spirit, miracles adjust the levels of perception and show them in proper alignment. This places spirit at the center, where it can communicate directly."

Here again is how Kingsolver describes Dellarobia's experience: "She was pressed by the quiet elation of escape and knowing better and seeing straight through to the back of herself, in solitude. She couldn't remember when she'd had such room for being."

Have you ever had such a room for being?

Essay 4

"Now you're talking crazy. Is this something religious?

Dellarobia is talking to her best friend, Dovey, a friend she has had since childhood, in whom she confides just about everything. She is telling Dovey about the planned tryst in the hunting cabin up on the mountain, and her assignation being disrupted by the sighting of the Monarch butterflies, and her spiritual epiphany of sorts.

"If I had a reasonable explanation, you would hear it, Dovey. This is all I can tell you: it wasn't my decision. Something happened. I was blind, but now I see."

"Now you're talking crazy. Is this something religious?"

Dellarobia was at pain to answer. In twenty years she had sheltered nothing from Dovey, but there were no regular words for this. *When you pass through the rivers they will not sweep over you. When you walk though fire, the flames will not set you ablaze.* That was the book of Isiah. "It's not religious," she said. p.33

Dellarobia has no explanation for what has happened to her, her epiphany. Dovey, frightened for her friend, says, "Is this something religious?" and Dellarobia, trying to reassure her friend, denies her experience, maybe a little embarrassed and says, "It's not religious."

In our world of intellectual materialism we are quick to deny and eschew a religious experience. We are afraid to admit it even when it hits us along side the head like a 2 x 4. We could explain this embarrassment and denial by immaturity. Dellarobia is young, only in her mid 20s. She is very caught up in the material world and the conventional norms of the society she has been conditioned by. She has yet to be aware that she is complicit in creating the hell of the life she is living in. Her awareness grows as the story continues but for now Life is scaring her out of her normal habit of thinking and doing but, as the text says, she is at a pain to answer Dovey's question of whether she is going crazy or religious, neither acceptable options to the two friends.

I had a serious bout of depression back in 2009, one that interfered with my functioning. I was anxious, very sad, couldn't sleep, couldn't concentrate, had, what is called, "an impending sense of doom". I thought I was physically sick with something like the flu. I felt like I was "coming down with something", but the illness never erupted. I just continued to feel anxious, depressed, and wanted to isolate,

10

withdraw, and not deal with anything. One of the things I perseverated on at the time was the dire predictions about climate change, and that we humans have crossed an important line and we are doomed. With the help of psychotherapy and anti-depressants, my depression and anxiety have lifted, but five years later, this sense of something very important happening to me still lingers. If you ask what troubled me so to bring this episode on I would be "at pain to answer". But like Dellarobia, I may be experiencing a prophetic moment when we are confronted by the "signs of the times" harkening a significant change in things to come.

For those who are spiritually sensitive, the fact that Gaia is groaning in pain has registered whether in a spiritual epiphany or a depression. And the only sane response in this insane world is to call for repentance. Human beings must acknowledge their sins, their mistakes, the error of their ways, and change. Dellarobia does repent. She tells Dovey that while she takes no credit something has graced her with the error of her former ways and now she senses a different and better path which she must proceed along even though she, at this point, can't make any sense of it. Dellarobia is bound to proceed on faith, faith in the truth of what is happening to her.

We Unitarian Universalists will need plenty of faith to proceed in the difficult times that are upon us. We will need each other and our principles more than ever and covenanting together to affirm and promote them is our hope that we can manage the future, as bad as it may become, in loving and constructive ways. Mother Nature asks this of us if we are to survive as a species unlike all the species that our irresponsible behavior have killed.

Essay 5

Money or butterflies, that is the question?

Bear Turnbow, Cub's father and Dellarobia's father-in-law, is planning on selling the trees in the woods that the Monarch butterflies are roosting in to loggers for money to pay his taxes and the balloon payment on his equipment loan. Not only is Bear planning on selling some of the trees, but he is planning on allowing the loggers to clear cut. Here is how Kingsolver writes the scene:

"A clear cut. Cub, honey, could you at least sit up and discuss this like a human? You mean they are taking out everything down to the slash?"

Cub sat up and gave her a sorry look. He has fleece clinging to his trousers and hay in his hair, a sight to see. "That's where they'll give you the most money. According to Dad, it's easier when they don't have to pick and choose the trees." p. 39

The bumper sticker says, "Good, fast, cheap. Pick two." The capitalistic ethic tells us that the most money is the goal, even if other values suffer. Americans like speed. They want things fast: food, cars, and services.

A little further, Kingsolver, describes Cub's personality. He is a nice guy but not the sharpest knife in the drawer, not the brightest bulb on the shelf.

"And there stood Cub, with his rock steady faith that she knew more than he did, in any situation outside of automotive repair. His bewildered sexual gratitude, as near a thing to religious awe as a girl of her station could likely inspire. These boyish things had made him lovable. But you can run out of gas on boyish, that was the thing. The message that

12

should be engraved in every woman's wedding band." p. 40

As you read further in the novel you will find that Dellarobia is much more inspiring for attributes other than her body, and yet these qualities that might inspire a "religious awe" are lost on people who are not mature enough to perceive them.

Dellarobia senses that there is more at stake in logging this mountain than money; we might be talking the extinction of a species, and this fact of the situation might lead one to question, "Who gives two hoots?"

Bear and his family need the money. They are poor people living on the edge. He needs to pay his taxes or he will lose his farm. He needs to make the balloon payment on his equipment loan or his equipment will be repossessed. Who cares about bugs?

You might think that, were people more aware, they might take up a collection to pay Bear's taxes and equipment loan and then there would be no need to log the woods for money. But alas who would organize such an effort, educate people on what is at stake, collect the money if people would donate it? Is this what a church would do if its members were so inclined or some environmental group? Whose responsibility is it , anyway? You can't leave it to the likes of Bear, Cub, and Hester Turnbow. Dellarobia is an outsider in this family, and feels she has been treated as such, but she is Cub's wife and the mother of Bear and Hester's grandchildren. Dellarobia has power she doesn't know she has and as the story progresses she becomes more and more aware of it, like so many of us are discovering in our own lives.

As Mother Teresa said, "Do not wait for leaders. Do it alone, person to person." As Dellarobia moves forward step by step she follows her faith in her growing awareness of what's right. She is bemused and perplexed herself about what is happening around her and to her own consciousness. What is it with these butterflies?

Essay 6

How will we deal with climate change: like sheep or mature men and women?

In the novel, Flight Behavior by Barbara Kingsolver, the main character, Dellarobia, has been helping with the sheep shearing on the farm where she and her husband, Cub, live along with Cub's parents, Bear and Hester. Dellarobia takes a break and looks out the hay mow door on the second floor of the barn at the newly shorn sheep. Here is how Kingsolver describes the scene:

"When she (Dellarobia) opened them (the hay mow doors) she looked down on the sheep milling around in the dusk, surprisingly slim and trim without their wool. Pastor Bobby at Hester's church spoke of Jesus looking down on his flock from on high, and it seemed apt: an all-knowing creator probably would find humans to be exactly the same kind of ignorant little dumb-heads as these sheep. Right now they were butting each other like crazy. Hester said head-butting was a flock's way of figuring out who was boss, so it was normal to some extent, but Dellarobia had noticed that shearing always left them wildly uncertain as to who was who." p. 41

This analogy of sheep to human beings seems keenly appropriate especially as it comes to the insanity that is contributing to climate change. Human beings are contributing to it and as the old line from the comic strip Pogo said, "We have met the enemy and he is us." Except climate change isn't about us vs. them, but will affect all of us rich and poor alike. Of course, the rich can insulate themselves longer by capturing resources to mitigate the negative consequences while the poor will be the first to suffer and die, but eventually, homo sapiens, along with many other species of animals and plants, will become extinct.

There will be a lot of head butting as the competition for land, food, and other goods increases because of the influences of our changing climate. There is no God to save us, and Mother Nature operates on the principle of Karma not benevolence. And so, like Dellarobia watching the newly shorn sheep, we are left to wonder how our climate changing will play out when the new pecking order gets established and new roles are developed for people to play leading us to be able to recognize the cast of characters one from another. Unlike sheep though we are conscious creatures who can influence to some extent our own fate and whether this new fate will be founded on love, compassion, and justice or on attack, jealousy, and oppression remains to be seen. It is in our hearts and hands as Unitarian Universalists to show the world that there is a better way.

Essay 7

Saint of sinner? The Lord works in strange ways

Dellarobia has gone up on the mountain for a tryst with her lover in a hunting shack when she first saw the Monarch butterflies, King Billies, as her mother-in-law Hester and Dellarobia's seven year old son, Preston, came to call them. When Cub announced to Dellarobia that his father, Bear, was planning to log the mountain for money to pay his taxes and balloon equipment loan, Dellarobia convinced Cub and he and his father should go up on the mountain to inventory the trees before signing the contract. Cub resisted saying it wasn't necessary, but Dellarobia finally shamed him into doing it so that he and his father had a clear understanding of what it was they were selling. Once Bear and Cub went up the mountain and saw the butterflies and returned to get Hester and Dellarobia and went up to see them again they were mystified. here is how Kingsolver describes the scene:

"Mother, Dad, listen here. This is a miracle. She had a vision of this."
Bear scowled. "The hell."
"No, Dad, she did. She foretold it. After the shearing we were up talking in the barn, and she vowed and declared we had to come up here. That's why I kept telling you we should. She said there was something big up here in our backyard."
Dellarobia felt the dread of her secrets. She recalled only her impatience, speaking to Cub in anger that night, telling him anything could be up here. Terrorists or blue trees."
Hester peered into her face as if trying to read in bad light. "Why would he say that? That you foretold it."

A paragraph later Kingsolver writes:

"Here's your vision. I see a meddling wife." Bear shook his head in weary disgust, a gesture that defined him, like the dog tags he still wore after everyone else had given up on his war. A large and mighty man among the triffling, that was Bear's drill. "You all need to get down off you high horses," he said. "We're going to spray these things and go ahead. I've got some DDD saved back in the basement."

The DDD was illegal, of course, having been banned after Rachel' Carson's book, "Silent Spring," convinced congress they had to do something to protect the environment from such a toxic insecticide.

As they argue with Bear about the judiciousness of killing the butterflies with DDD, Cub finally says to Bear:

"Listen. Dad. There's a reason for everything."

16

"That's true, Bear," Hester said. "This could be the Lord's business."

*Cub seemed to flinch, turning to Dellarobia. "That's what **she** said. We should come and have a look, because it was the Lord's business."*

And the plot thickens as they say. Dellarobia lets her husband and mother and father-in- law think that she has a vision inspired by the Lord about the butterflies. Little did anyone guess that she had actually seen them on her way to commit adultery. What some might judge the work of the devil has been flipped into the work of the Lord and instead of a sinner, Dellarobia, is perceived as something akin to a modern day saint having visions of the wholeness of the planet and the need to protect a species endangered by climate change.

The Lord does work in mysterious ways. Who would have thought that the Lord might have used what humans think of as sexual sin to protect the victims of environmental sin. Perhaps the god of Mother Nature is not the same god as the god of the old testament. Jesus let the adulterous woman go from the guilty verdict of those who would have executed her for her crime while those who destroy the fabric of Mother Nature knowingly and willing may be guilty of far greater crimes than ones of simple carnal lust. The harm that is done to Mother Nature and its negative consequences for the people who are victimized is far, far greater, than any harm done by indulging one's personal and private lust.

And so is Dellarobia a sinner or a saint or like most of us, perhaps, a little of both?

Co-creating with God the future of the planet Dellarobia, Cub, Hester, Bear, and Bear's friend, Norm are still up on the mountain taking in the marvel of the butterfly roost in the trees intended for logging.

Bear exhaled a hiss of doubt. "What if they don't fly off?"

"I don't know." Cub still held onto Dellarobia by the shoulders. "Y'all just need to see the Lord's hand in this and trust in His bidding. Like she said."

At the end of this chapter, Chapter 2, there is quite a moving passage:

"Hester's eyes dropped from her son's face to Dellarobia's, and what could possibly happen next, she had no idea. For years she'd couched on a corner of this farm without really treading into Turnbow family territory, and now here she stood, dead in its center. She felt vaguely like a hostage in her husband's grip, as if police megaphones might come out and the bullets would fly. Looking down at her feet made her dizzy, because butterfly shadows rolling like pebbles along the floor of a fast stream. The illusion of current knocked her off balance. She raised her eyes to the sky instead, and that made the others look up too, irresistibly led, even Bear. Together they saw light streaming through glowing wings. Like embers, she thought, a flood of fire, the warmth they had craved so long. She felt her breathing rupture again into laughter or sobbing in her chest, sharp, vocal exhalations she couldn't contain. The sounds coming out of her veered toward craziness.

The two older men stepped back as if she'd slapped them.

'Lord almighty, the girl is receiving 'grace,' said Hester, and Dellarobia could not contradict her."p. 56-57

It seems not only Dellarobia, but they all are receiving grace as they wonder and marvel at the phenomenon of Mother Nature and must confront the choices involved in competing with other species for the scarce resources that all these species need for survival on this planet.

Humans, because of their consciousness and power of free will, have a greater responsibility for caring for the environment of the planet than other creatures. God has given us humans, the god like power to create or destroy. Cub tells his father, Bear, that they should trust in God's bidding, and not egotistically just destroy the habitat of another species for their own personal gain, money.

As we move into a geological era of the planet earth some have called the anthropocene, a geological era in which homo sapiens will determine the evolution of Gaia's development, we need to raise our consciousnesses so we can not only make wise choices, but change our patterns of living on earth to be respectful of the interdependent dynamics that maintain and promote good health and well being for all species.

The "grace" that has befallen Dellarobia and the others is the dawning awareness of a huge responsibility and partnership with God for the well being of God's creation. In their little corner of the world, on their mountain, will they be up to the task? Are we, in our own little corners of the world, up to the task?

Essay 8

The seed of reverence is born

Kingsolver writes in Flight Behavior:

"So she was what Hester called a 911 Christian; in the event of an emergency, call the Lord. Unlike all those who called on Jesus daily rain or shine, to discuss their day and feel the love. Once upon a time, she'd had a mother for that. Jesus was a more reliable backer, evidently, less likely to drink himself unconscious or get liver cancer. No wonder people chose Him as their number-one friend. But if the chemistry wasn't there, what could you do? Dellarobia scrutinized life too hard, she knew that. For a year she'd gone with Cub to Wednesday Bible group and loved the sense of going back to school, but her many questions did not make her the teacher's pet." p.61

It is written in the second chapter of A Course In Miracles: "Tolerance for pain may be high, but it is not without limit. Eventually everyone begins to recognize, however, dimly, that there must be a better way. As this recognition becomes more firmly established, it becomes a turning point." ACIM, T-2.III.3.:5-7

This may be the Course's version of what Hester calls the 911 Christian.

As it is written in the Perennial Philosophy by Aldous Huxley:

"...it is, for very many persons, much easier to behave selflessly in time of crisis that it is when life is taking its normal course in undisturbed tranquility. When the going is easy, there is nothing to make us forget our precious selfness, nothing (except our own will to mortification and knowledge of God) to distract our minds from the distractions with which we have chosen to be identified; we are at perfect liberty to wallow in our personality to our heart's content. And how we wallow!" p.42

Osho says that the first step on a truly spiritual path is rebellion, questioning. As Rev. Galen Guengerich tells his story, when he left the Mennonite community of his upbringing and went to seminary, many members of the church worried he would lose his faith. Guengerich writes that he didn't lose *his* faith but the faith of his family of origin.

Dellarobia is an adult child of an alcoholic and has learned to be skeptical of authority figures like her mother, because her alcoholic mother could not be relied upon, depended on, trusted. Dellarobia has learned from an early age to survive by her own wits and so while she is encouraged to believe, and wants to believe, as she puts it "the chemistry" wasn't there and what could she do? Then, the butterflies appear while she is engaged in the pursuit of what she has been taught is sinful, and she has an awakening which she still doesn't know to what it will be, but she has become aware that there must be a better way, that she is being called to a better way, a better self.

Many of us, I expect have had experiences like this probably born out of crisis and tragedy of some kind as well. Most of us are nudged to look deeper at the meaning of life at the 911 moments in our life. It is in our suffering that Unitarian Universalism has something to offer, not in terms of required beliefs, creeds, dogmas, but in terms of values upon which to create and develop a happy life. Dellarobia is becoming awakened to the seventh principle of Unitarian Universalism, the interdependent web of existence of which we are a part and all the awesome mystery that implies which begs for the development and assumption of a reverent attitude towards self, others, and the world.

Essay 9

Venal or precious, secular or holy?

From Chapter 4 of Flight Behavior by Barbara Kingsolver:

"I didn't mind when it was just people from church coming up," Hester complained to Valia, "but now everybody and his dog wants the grand tour. After it came out in the paper. It was about thirty of them up her the Friday after Thanksgiving. I want to tell you! That's not normal, for the day after Thanksgiving."

"No, it isn't." Valia agreed. "People should be at the mall." p. 77

Laugh if you want but this is portrayed as serious conversation between two working class, white, women in Tennessee who have bought into the American dream of rampant materialism and the holiest of High Holy Days, Black Friday, is being eschewed in favor of tramping up a mountain side to view the winter roost of a wonder of nature, Monarch Butterflies. To the worshipers of Mammon this appears blasphemous and sacrilegious. We have become so inured to our materialistic values that this behavior of communing with nature and reverencing the works of Mother Nature seems unnatural and dysfunctional and both Hester and Valia agree that going to see butterflies instead of to the mall the day after Thanksgiving doesn't seem natural.

However the venal impulse and mercenary values are so deeply ingrained that Crystal says to Hester, "Here's what you ought to do, about all these people coming up? You should charge them."

"See, that's what I told Bear," Hester said. "We both think that."

"What's stopping you, then?" Valia asked.

Hester raised her eyebrows and pointed her chin at Dellarobia, as if her daughter-in-law were a child, oblivious to the codes of adults.

"Hey, don't look at me. Your son's the one that spilled the beans in church, blame him." Dellarobia got up and dumped an armload of tied bundles into the sink. Brethren, fix your thoughts on what is true. Bobby's (the pastor) words came to her out of the blue, and she nearly spoke them aloud. Instead, she said, "Let's blame Bobby Ogle, while we're at it. And Jesus, why not Jesus? Credit where credit is due."

"Missy, you are asking for it with talk like that."

22

"It's Mrs. And you know what? I *never* said it's the Lord's divine hand at work up there. Go ahead and charge people if you want. Why wouldn't you?

Hester met her eye, and they held a moment in deadlock. The words *born again* rose to Dellarobia's mind, and she contemplated a world where Hester no longer scared her. To turn her back on permanent rebuke, and find motives for living, wouldn't that be something. Like living as a no-heller, as Bobby was said to be." pp.81-82

The worlds of Mammon and Mother Nature, venal and precious, secular and holy collide and while Dellarobia won't take full responsibility but deflects it onto Bobby Ogle, the pastor, and sarcastically onto Jesus she none the less somehow finds the courage to stand up to her mother-in-law by whom, previously, she had always felt intimidated, and assert a different view based on different values than those of her mother-in-law and the materialistic, secular world she found herself ensconced in.

While on one level it seems like an important and reasonable thing to do, protect the habitat of the butterflies, human beings have been used to the idea for the last 2,000 years, and especially the last 200 since the advent of the industrial age, that it's all about them and the environment be damned. It is there simply for the pleasure and the profit of human beings, and God, in the story of Genesis, has given homo sapiens the permission to dominate Mother Nature to their will and to do with her as they would including pillage and rape. These women appear to have an intuitive inkling that this attitude is corrupt and evil and, while they discuss the possibility of taking monetary advantage of the situation, they feel guilty in the presence of Dellarobia, and the religious and spiritual discourse which has been brought to the situation.

Jesus has said in Mark 6:36, "What good is it if a person

23

gains the whole world, but forfeits his or her soul?"

As Unitarian Universalists, a people of faith, we get the point, we see the issue, we reverence the interdependent web at least in our words if not always in our actions. Would UUs stand with Dellarobia in solidarity, be supportive of her newly found values, be a witness to the quandary the women, the Turnbow family, the community, and the world find themselves in? I would hope so, and hope is an important initial motivation for faith as one embarks on a new and better path even if it is not always clear where this path is taking the person.

Essay 10

Mercy and repentance are appropriate at this time in the planet's history.

Dellarobia's son, Preston, goes to kindergarten where he has met a classmate, Josefina Delgado, who is a daughter in a migrant farm family from Michoacan, Mexico where the Monarchs usually go to roost in the winter time until flooding caused landslides that not only destroyed their traditional roosting site but also the village where the Delagados lived as well.

The Delagados had heard about the Monarchs on the Turnbow property from their daughter and came to visit Dellarobia hoping they could climb the mountain and see the butterflies. Only the daughter, Josefina, speaks any English and Dellarobia speaks no Spanish, so Josefina translates for the adults as Dellarobia learn their story. The chapter ends with this paragraph:

"They all sat quietly for a long time. Dellarobia had ridden out prayer meetings aplenty, but had no idea what to say to a

24

family that had lost their world, including the mountain under their feet and the butterflies of the air." p. 103

Indeed what does one say in the face of ecological devastation. The grief is palpable but unspoken as it is so fresh and new as to be mind numbing and unbelievable. And yet, here, through the facilitation of their 6 year olds, they grapple with the phenomenon which they literally don't have the words to share with one another because they don't speak each other's languages, but even it they did, they would still find their words unsatisfactory in describing the enormity of what they have witnessed and lived through.

With hubris, human beings have been polluting the planet and Mother Nature is not pleased. Those of us old enough to have adult children and grandchildren and maybe even great grand children will not live long enough to see the consequences of our insensitive behavior but our grand children and great grand children certainly will, and we should be ardently praying for mercy, and as best we are able, repenting for our sins.

Essay 11

Can we depend on the proponents of predatory capitalism to save us?

Dr. Ovid Byron is the entomologist from California who has come to Tennessee to study the butterflies. He has set up his lab in Cub and Dellarobia's barn behind their house and even hired Dellarobia as an assistant and she is getting a lot of on the job training. One day, they are up on the mountain, collecting data on the butterflies and they take a lunch break and have a discussion about how climate change is not only affecting the butterflies but life on the planet. They are talking about the carbon in the atmosphere and how it contributes to a warming of the temperature of the planet.

Here is part of how Kingsolver writes the scene:

"If you stop something, it stops," she said, sounding a little too fine.

"We used to think so. But there are unstoppable processes. Like the loss of polar ice. White ice reflects the heat of the sun directly back to space. But when it melts, the dark land and water underneath hold on to the heat. The frozen ground melts. And that releases more carbon into the air. These feedback loops keep surprising us."

How could this be true, she thought, if no one was talking about it? People with influence. Important people made such a big deal over infinitely smaller losses.

"So it's not a question of having Floridian winters in Tennessee," he said. "That's not even under discussion."

"Is there some part of this I can actually see?"

"You don't believe in things you can't see?"

She thought of Blancie Bise and Bible class. The flood of Noah, Jesus. She did try. "It's never been my long suit," she confessed.

"Your children's adulthood?"

That nearly floored her of course. Or creeked her. Since that's what was below this log, if she'd swooned off of it. How dare he belt her with that one?

"A trend is intangible, but real," he said calmly. "A photo cannot prove a child is growing, but several of them show the change over time. Align them, and you can reliably predict what is coming. You never see it all at once. An attention

26

span is required." pp.279-280

Ah, yes, an attention span is required, something that Americans with the 24 hour cable tv news cycle, social media, texting, etc. don't possess. We go through our days with blinders on from one task to the next, pursuing one desire after another, distracting ourselves with all kinds of drama to keep our minds off of the low level anxiety which rumbles constantly in our psyches as we attempt to deny the karma which we generate on an hour to hour and day to day basis which will hold us accountable not only for our guilty pleasures but for an irresponsible life style we take for granted and even feel entitled to.

And Dellarobia, like an innocent child wonders to herself, why people with influence, our leaders, the people who we depend on to lead us and take care of us, haven't concerned themselves with this impending planetary catastrophe. Good question! And the answer is...........................

There are more immediate incentives and concerns like campaign contributions from fossil fuel corporations who lobby congress for policies and laws that enhance their bottom line based on the values of what Noam Chomsky called predatory capitalism. Protecting the commons, the air we breath, the climate of our planet is what the economists call an externality that interferes with the financial bottom line.

Every day people like Cub and Dellarobia, Hester and Bear, Dovey and Crystal have no idea what is being done to them, but Dellarobia is waking up. She senses something isn't right, and Dr. Bryon, a scientist, not a theologian or a philosopher of ethics, is sharing with her the science of what is happening which tells us truths contrary to the values of predatory capitalism and corporations, who, feeling financially threatened by the awakening to the truth, are cranking up the

27

engines of what Shane Kuhn, in his novel, The Intern's
Handbook, calls the Bull Shit express.

Like the disinformation campaign of the tobacco companies
when science began to show that smoking caused cancer, the
fossil fuel corporations are engaging in a disinformation
campaign of climate change denial. Dellarobia is losing her
innocence. Her naivete is giving way to disillusionment, and
she begins to question why, if what the science says is
happening, is really happening, the adults in our society on
whom we would like to depend, have not been taking this
information more seriously to protect us.

Unitarian Universalists covenant together to affirm and
promote the seventh principle, a respect for the
interdependent web of existence, and in order to do this we
need to have a right understanding of the world we are just a
small part of, and this requires the application of the UU
fourth principle, the free and responsible search for truth and
meaning. Dellarobia is a lukewarm evangelical Christian but
she is awakening to the significance of the Unitarian
Universalist principles. Dellarobia is growing and it is in the
honor and privilege to witness her growth, and we begin to
have hope in the face of a growing sense of impending doom.

Essay 12

Sitting the death vigil for the extinction of a species

Dellarobia and Dr. Ovid Byron are up on the mountain
collecting data. It had been cold the night before and there is
a question of whether the roosting Monarch butterflies will
survive. As the day warms up, melting occurs and it rains.
They are standing under a tent like canopy to shelter a small

work space. Here is how Kingsovler describes it:

Long clusters of butterflies began to drip. Hangers-on at the bottoms of their strings twisted slowly in an imperceptible wind, like the caricature of a hanged man. A chunk of a cluster near the shelter dropped suddenly to the ground, severed from the great beast. Grounded butterflies could not hope to lift themselves in a rain like this. She watched this fresh legion of the extinguished, taking their time to die.

"Nobody else came to the site today?" she asked.

He shook his head.

"I've left a couple of messages with Vern, but he doesn't call back. It seems like we're losing volunteers. Maybe they're having exams."

Ovid said, "Not everyone has the stomach to watch an extinction."

She noticed the fabric over their heads had begun to droop in spots where the rain pooled. The roof of their invisible house, collapsing. What wouldn't, under all this. She was slowly submitting to his sense that weather is everything. Not just the moving-picture view out the window. Real, in a way that the window and the house were not.

A scattering of butterflies in the fallen mass twitched open and closed, while getting pounded, showing their vivid orange a few last times. 'Rage, rage against the dying light.' That was the end of a poem, brought to her by the one bright spot in her education, Mrs. Lake, now dead.
Dellarobia suddenly found she could scarcely bear this day at all. She stepped out in the rain to pick up one of the pitiful survivors and bring it under their roof. She held it close to her face. A female. And ladylike, with its slender velvet

abdomen, its black eyes huge and dolorous. The probocis curled and uncurled like a spring. She could feel the hooked tips of the threadlike legs while they gripped her finger. She held it out and the wings opened wide, a small signal.

"So you're one of the people that can," she said. "Watch an extinction."

He did not quite break his communion with the day, his vigil, whatever it was, but asked, "If someone you loved was dying, what would you do?"
pp. 318-319

Most of us don't have the the stomach to watch an extinction so we watch sports, movies, anything to distract us from the reality of what is happening to our planet caused by us humans. We are in the geological age which Eugene Stoermer called the Anthropocene indicating the significant influence that human activity is having on the planet. Once we acknowledge and understand what the scientists are telling us about our impact, we have increasing responsibility to manage our relationship with the interdependent web in constructive, empathic, and loving ways.

Dr. Ovid Byron is sitting vigil over the possible extinction of a species, Monarch butterflies, which is happening at increasingly frequent rates to other species as well. The biodiversity of planet earth is being decreased and eroded because of the activity of one species, homo sapiens. The difference between our species and others is that we have consciousness, we know what we are doing if we choose to pay attention and take responsibility.

There is no other religious denomination that has the moral awareness of Unitarian Universalists of the relationship of human beings with the interdependent web other than Native American and Wiccan. We have ensconced our awareness

30

and values in our seventh principle of respecting the interdependent web of existence of which homo sapiens is just a part. Unitarian Universalists, based on our faith, need to enhance our light to the world on the rightness of the respect and collaboration with Gaia if we are to survive as a species and continue to be the co-creators with God of the world being created.

We can sit the death vigil with Dr. Byron and express our grief for our sins, but this has little value unless we also repent and change the way we live on this planet. As Unitarian Universalist preachers are fond of saying, "May it be so."

Essay 13

Studying climate change is the work of science not the work of conscience.

Dr. Ovid Byron is an entomologist, a scientist, and he, patiently, explains to Dellarobia, the role of science in our contemporary world.

"I am not a zookeeper," he said. "I'm not here to save monarchs. I'm trying to read what they are writing on our wall."

Dellarobia felt stung. "If you're not, who is?" She could think of some answers: the knitting women, the boys with duct-taped clothes. People Cub and her in-laws thought to be outside the pale of normal adulthood.

"That is a concern of conscience," he said. "Not of biology. Science doesn't tell us what we should do. It only tells us what is."

"That must be why people don't like it," she said, surprised at her tartness.

Ovid, too, seemed startled. "They don't like science?"

"I'm sorry. I'm probably speaking out of turn here. You've explained to me how big this is. The climate thing. That it's taking our stuff we're counting on. But other people say just forget it. My husband, guys on the radio. They say it's not proven."

"What we're discussing is clear and present, Dellarobia. Scientists agree on that. These men on the radio, I assume, are nonscientists. Why would people buy snake oil when they want medicine?"

"That's what I'm trying to tell you. You guys aren't popular. Maybe your medicine's too bitter. Or you're not selling us. Maybe you're writing us off, thinking we won't get it. You should start with kindergartners and work your way up."

"It's too late for that. Believe me."

"Don't say that, 'too late.' I hate that. I've got my kids to think about." pp.320-321

Dellarobia is thinking about her children, 6 year old Preston in kindergarten, and toddler, Cordie. Are we adults thinking of our children, our grandchildren, our great grandchildren and beyond? Not much. We've found Rush Limbaugh and the other climate change deniers very attractive because we don't want to believe the science and imagine the world we are leaving the people coming after us.

Climate change is not the same thing as weather as most intelligent people know, but less intelligent people only know what is happening to their bodies, they don't think abstractly enough to understand things they can't see. Fossil fuel corporations have a field day with these concrete thinkers who regurgitated trivial information for their exams in high school and college to get a good grade, but never developed the skills of critical thinking and analysis.

Using Fowler's stages of religious development, I would guess that most UUs, especially those who have converted, are at the higher stages of development indicated by attitudes of curiosity instead of certainty, systems thinking instead of linear, reductive cause and effect thinking, and tolerance of ambiguity instead of black and white concrete conclusions. People at lower stages of faith development believe in supernatural gods who control the universe and reward good and bad behavior of people on earth. They often perceive themselves as God's children whom God, as a parent, should take care of and protect from themselves.

We are at a time in our evolutionary process when human beings need to grow up and Dr. Byron is clear with Dellarobia that the role of science is to report the data and the facts. What people do with that information is determined by another realm, one of values, morals and ethics, the realm usually thought of as religion or as Dr. Byon puts it, "conscience". Science, Dr. Byron, says tells us what is, not what we should do.

And Unitarian Universalism is pretty clear about what we should do although I am not sure, given where our evolutionary path has taken us, that it is enough. The seventh principle says that UUs covenant to affirm and promote the *respect* for the interdependent web of existence of which we are a part. Perhaps it should say to *protect* and respect.....

Dellarobia in a child-like way wants the scientists to protect us from the climate change they are reporting as if they were gods or some sort of modern day super heroes who will, with magic powers, tame the weather and save life on the globe. But alas, scientists are objective, and study phenomena. "It is what it is" as the Buddhists say. What should be done about what is, and what is wanted, is based on another kind of knowledge: values. What should we value? What is the Good Life and how do we create it? The story describing that is the work of religion. As Unitarian Universalists we have a lot of work to do to tell our story and promote our values in a world that often seems deaf and blind.

Essay 14

Unitarian Universalism is a religion for the mature, the courageous, the brave

Dr. Ovid Byron, the entomologist's wife, Juliet, an anthropologist, has come from California to visit with her husband as he does his field work on the Monarch butterflies in Tennessee. The couple is having dinner with Dellarobia and Cub, a professional middle class couple, with a farming couple 20 years their junior.

Kingsolver writes:

*Ovid was explaining something to Juliet that he called the theory of the territorial divide. With some confusion, Dellarobia understood this was **her** theory, he was attributing it to her, though the terms he used were unfamiliar: climate-change denial functioned like folk art for some people, he said, a way of defining survival in their own terms. But it's not indigenous, Juliet argued. It's like a cargo cult. Introduced from the outside, corporate motives via conservative media. But now it's become fully identified with the icons of local culture, so it's no longer up for discussion.*

34

"The key thing is," Juliet said, resting her elbow on the table, that beautiful wrist bending under the weight of its wooden rings, "once you're talking identity, you can't lecture that out of people. The condescension of outsiders won't diminish it. That just galvanizes it."

Dellarobia felt abruptly conscious of her husband and her linoleum. "Christ on the cross," she said without enthusiasm. "The rebel flag, mud flaps, science illiteracy. That would be us."

"I am troubled by this theory, Dellarobia," Ovid said, "but I can't say you are wrong. I've read a lot of scholarly articles on the topic, but you make more sense."

*"Well, **yeah**," Juliet said, "that's kind of the point, that outsiders won't get it."* p.395

Most human beings although they benefit from the knowledge and technology gained from science are scientifically illiterate. The skill of scientific thinking and problem analysis has never been acquired by most people as a result of their education to facilitate a higher level of more deliberate and purposeful functioning. Most people still function based on emotional responses to what they perceive as external circumstances fueled by unconscious conditioning based on the avoidance, containment, or elimination of fear.

The avoidance, containment, and, if possible, the elimination of fear, is achieved by the security of belonging to a group of like minded people who will have your back and help protect you. Identification with the group, it's symbols, rules, values, beliefs, practices becomes important, so the individual thinks and feels, for survival. And yet we live in a time where "group think", especially if the "group think" is wrong, is especially important for the survival of the whole species of homo sapiens.

Juliet seems to be saying that correct understanding, right mindedness, must come from within the group, because if the group perceives the attempts to change their "group think" as coming from without, they will just feel threatened and become more "galvanized".

What is the Unitarian Univeralist approach to people caught up in "group think"? It advocates in its fourth principle the "free and responsible search for truth and meaning" but not many people have the temperament, or the maturity, to be what are called "free thinkers". Perhaps it is the fifth principle, "the right of conscience and the use of the democratic process within our congregations and in society at large" which has the best utility in this situation of dysfunctional "group think". I was taught as a Roman Catholic that my conscience was the final arbiter of right and wrong. To be right with God meant that I was to bring my conscience into compliance with what I thought and felt God was calling to me to do. As long as I went with my conscience I would be all right. As St. Paul says in his letter to Corinthians, "If God is with you, who can be against you." It was my discernment of the will of God, not the group, that was to be used as the final guide to my choices and decisions.

The psychological consideration is whether the individual is mature enough, has the courage, is brave enough to stand up for his or her conscience? If not he or she may go along with the group out of fears of punishment, being dismissed as crazy, or exile and excommunication for rocking the boat, going against the grain, disturbing the status quo, stepping on the toes of the leaders of group who have the power to enforce compliance.

Unitarian Universalism is not a religion for the weak, the cowardly, the insecure, the people pleasers. We understand that our environment is being changed by human activity and

36

that species are being made extinct and the weather is changing leading to significant changes in the geological functioning of our planet. The moral question is whether we, homo sapiens, will take responsibility or continue with the same because of the short term profit and security of the familiar?

What is happening to our climate is a matter of science. What should be done about the changes that science is learning about is a matter of ethics. The ethical base for Unitarian Universalism articulated in its seven principles can be the saving grace for all species at this time in our geological evolution of this planet. Will we be a light unto the world, the yeast in the dough, the salt of the earth?

Essay 15

Flight Behavior: The moral of the story

At the end of Flight Behavior by Barbara Kingsolver, Dellarobia, and her 6 year old son, Preston, leave the house to walk to the neighbor's peach orchard where the butterflies have descended off the mountain roost temporarily in the cold snowy weather. It is early in the morning when Preston is waiting for the school bus to take him to his kindergarten and Dellarobia has decided this is the time to tell Preston that she and Cub are separating and that they will be moving to an apartment.

"Why did you and Dad get married by accident?" he asked.
"People do wrong things all the time, Preston. Grown-ups. You're going to find that out. You will be amazed. There's some kind of juice in our brains that makes us only care about what's right in front of us right this minute. Even if we know something different will happen later and we should think about that too. Our brains trick us. They say:

37

Fight this thing right now, or run away from it. Tomorrow doesn't matter, dude."

He stopped strumming his knee, and appeared to think this over.

"If I could teach you one thing, Preston, that's it. Think about what's coming at you later. But see, all parents say that to all kids. We don't follow our own advice."

He sat perfectly still, staring at snow.

"You know what else? Grown-ups will never admit what I just told you. They'll basically poop their own beds without saying they made a mistake, even the ones that think they are A-number-one good citizens. They'll lie there saying, 'Hey, I didn't make this mess, somebody else pooped this bed.'"

The tiniest of smiles pulled his mouth out of line, like a snag in a stocking.

"You and Cordie are going to grow up in some deep crap, let me tell you. You won't even get a choice. You'll have to be different." p.428

When we finish Flight Behavior we can ask, "And what is the moral of the story? What is the lesson to learn from this novel? What meaning did you make of the story?"

First, Barbara Kingsolver is a gifted writer. I have loved all her books, both fiction and non-fiction. Flight Behavior grapples with difficult subjects: climate change, stagnating marriages, fears for the future for children we desperately love, the role of science in society, the role of ethics in society, the dynamics of extended family life, cultural differences of region and class, infidelity, the importance of friendship, and the role of religion in our contemporary society. Whew! This is not a beach read but a novel of substance, depth, elegance, grace, and challenge.

Second, Flight Behavior deals with the most significant and challenging topic of our contemporary times, climate change which will affect all of us on the planet in very significant ways over the coming decades and centuries. The science is not debatable at this point, 99% of scientists agree with it, climate change is happening at a rapid rate and it is human induced. Those with vested interests want to argue because they don't want their profits threatened, or their life style disrupted, their political power, or some other vested interest disturbed.

Third, the major moral of the story is one of hope, that humans grow, can become more aware, that they can adjust and respond positively to what some might experience as negative changes. While Dellarobia is concerned for her children's future she is confident that Preston will grow up into a good man, and Cordie into a good woman, who will benefit humankind and life on the planet. What Dellarobia, herself, will do with the next stage of her life is unclear, but she is bright, capable, earnest, and with a sense of purpose has given up her adolescent sexual acting out in service of being true to herself and her desire to be of service to the other creatures on the planet.

Fourth, the lesson of the story is that we, as humans, need to grow-up and take responsibility for ourselves and our environment. Some of us have grown-up, some of us like Dellarobia are in process, and some of us need to get with the program if we are to salvage some semblance of civilization on the planet. It is time to give up childish things, and thinking, and behavior. As St. Paul wrote in his first letter to the Corinthians, chapter 13, verse 11, "When I was a child, I talked like a child, I thought like a child, I reasoned like a child. When I became a man, I put the ways of childhood behind me."

What does it take to grow-up and put away the things of a child? Education, instruction, guidance, and accountability. Who will provide it? Religion for our modern age. Just one religion or a particular one? It will take them all, working together in an interreligious collaboration, to save ourselves, each other, and as much life as we can on this planet in its multitudinous diversity. For me Unitarian Universalism works best with its seven principles and its Christian history with a little Buddhism and humanism thrown in with some Wiccan and Native Spirituality, and Sufism, and Hindu stuff. In short, my God is too big for any one religion. The teaching of Flight Behavior is that we humans can't screw with Mother Nature arrogantly without suffering her displeasure.

However, being aware, and respectful, and full of compassion for ourselves, other living things, and the planet, we can transform our functioning in ways that will protect Gaia, love Mother Nature, and nurture Her creatures as best we can even Her butterflies.

This book is the second in a series of book of the month reflections on the UU A Way Of Life on - line magazine. Many of the ideas articulated here may also be of benefit to people who do not consider themselves Unitarian Universalist.

For further copies of this book and other books by David G. Markham search by his name on Amazon.com

It is a privilege for the author to have you read and consider the ideas expressed here. If you have comments and ideas please contact the author using the information below.

David G. Markham
46 King Street
Brockport, NY 14420
585-727-3663
davidgmarkham@gmail.com

You also might be interested in the author's blog, UU A Way Of Life, where articles and videos are usually posted daily.

www.uuawayoflife.blogspot.com

CPSIA information can be obtained at www.ICGtesting.com
Printed in the USA
BVOW03s1756011214

377435BV00019B/549/P